Waiting
for a Miracle

Waiting for a Miracle

Asa. 49:13

Jan Markell

Jan Markell

Baker Books

A Division of Baker Book House Co.
Grand Rapids, Michigan 49516

© 1993 by Jan Markell

Published by Baker Books
a division of Baker Book House Company
P.O. Box 6287, Grand Rapids, MI 49516-6287

ISBN: 0-8010-6297-7

Printed in the United States of America

This book is dedicated to all who have visible and invisible affliction. It is also dedicated to June Moline. In spite of her own debilitating affliction, she has never grown weary of my weariness.

Contents

Strengthen the feeble hands,
  steady the knees that give way;
say to those with fearful hearts,
  Be strong, do not fear;
your God will come . . .
  he will come to save you.

(Isa. 35:3–4)

Foreword

Start with the hearer! Always start with the hearer!" insisted my old homiletics professor as he struggled to teach us fledgling preachers to communicate the gospel to real human beings. We seminarians were full to the brim with the truth that sets people free, but we didn't understand how to help people receive it. When we finally listened to this fundamental rule, the people we preached to were enabled to use the truth we had for them.

What makes *Waiting for a Miracle* so powerful is this: Jan Markell, who herself awaits a miracle, tells the truth so the reader can use it. And she does this by beginning where the suffering, chronically ill reader is. She doesn't start where God is, up high above us in wondrous beauty, wholeness, and perfection. She starts where we poor sinners are when we are sick, sometimes chronically sick, sometimes sicker for the belief that we have no hope of getting better. Then she takes the reader with her to where the truth flows pure and lovely to set free and to heal.

. "That's me!" you will say as you recognize your own complaint—your observation that God is so silent, or that this illness is such a waste, or that you certainly have waited a long time for help, or that it's hard to face the future, and so on. You're hooked because you know Jan knows how you feel and that therefore these devotions will help you.

How does she know? you'll catch yourself thinking! *How does she know exactly how I feel and what I think about as I lie here?* It's important for you to know the answer. Jan understands because she herself has been coping for weary years with what has come to be called "chronic fatigue syndrome" (CFS). With Jan, the syndrome began before medical science had a name for it. Doctors hadn't even acknowledged its existence and routinely referred those suffering from CFS to psychiatrists or psychologists. Then in the summer of 1989, she was one of 2,000 Americans poisoned by contaminants in a batch of L-Tryptophan, resulting for her in yet another layer of chronic illness! Jan has had to face the fact that she could not get out of bed to keep speaking engagements. She has had to cope with the sad truth that not much is known about cure for her ailments. She has had to endure the frustration of knowing God's call on her life—a call to be up

and doing—and at the same time, a nearly total inca-
pacity to perform. Thus it is that Jan understands how
it is with her readers.

But that isn't all. She has discovered what helps and
she leads us to discover it too. For instance, she tells
how our lives, though laid low by illness, can become
meaningful, worthwhile, anything but wasted. Answer:
let God's intention be carried out that the illness drive
us to him! She even shows us how to find meaning and
value in simply getting a diagnosis. Answer: when
we've suffered from some unknown disease, a diagnosis legitimates our illness and validates it so we don't
have to be brought even lower by nagging guilt and
torturing self doubt ("Am I making this up? Am I baby-
ing myself? Am I just trying to escape my duties?"). As
you read and pray through this book, you will learn
how to take one day at a time—even ten minutes at a
time for some people! You will learn about keeping
your balance among the demands of your condition,
your life, your duties, and your therapeutic regimen.
You will find help in forming realistic expectations of
the healthy others you live among.

Each devotion includes, besides Jan's own deeply
spiritual discoveries of truth, thought-provoking
examples of wisdom in suffering gleaned from the
writings of others and, especially helpful, a prayer in
poetic form which puts into words what the reader
wants to say to the Lord in Jesus' name.

A final word. It is my belief that, even as illness can
be made worse by telling ourselves negative, misbe-

lieving, hopeless self-statements ("I don't deserve this and it's unfair and unjust that I should be sick!" "God can't love me very much seeing he treats me like this!" "It's hopeless and I'll never get better!" "As long as I'm sick, I'll have to be miserable!" "Nobody else understands!" etc.), telling yourself the truth as it comes from Jesus Christ and his Word will move a person's body, mind, and spirit along the road toward healing, reconstruction, and a positive outcome even while turning affliction creatively into something worthwhile. This book will help you to make the most of the suffering God has allowed into your life!

William Backus

Introduction

Most would agree that health is the greatest wealth. There are many crises in life, and yet if we are in good health, we can usually fight the enemy and the circumstances. We can bounce back to a productive life.

Just as war transforms borders and boundaries, so the battle of affliction changes the entire course of our lives. This can be true for a short-term illness, and it is most certainly true of chronic illness. Illness opens up a Pandora's box of the unexpected and raises questions we never thought to ask. Can we survive this unwelcome visitor? Will loved ones abandon us? How long will it last? How much will it cost? Will life ever again be the same?

This is a devotional book about affliction and for the afflicted. It is not, however, a book that will dwell on despair. It is written to give insight and hope to victims of short- and long-term illness and to all who relate to them. Because God loves us, he has sent special people into our lives to make the journey into darkness brighter. They include friends, family members, and the select group of people often called caretakers. I think caretakers are for trees and shrubs, so I'd like to use the term Edith Schaeffer uses—*undershepherds*. They are God's anointed and appointed.

There are undershepherds and then there are the critics of the afflicted. There's a growing movement within Christianity that suggests it is unspiritual to become ill because illness may be related to poor spiritual temperature or lack of faith. When the afflicted person can get no relief through the health care system and when even prayer seems to bounce off the ceiling, tremendous guilt and shame can be heaped on that sick believer. It's the proverbial last straw. And it does *nothing* to help that person become well and whole again. The Bible states clearly that all believers will suffer persecution, affliction, and various "thorns" throughout life. But these hurdles can be overcome, and I trust this book will help some victims of infirmity do just that! Many readers will have followed a diligent prescribed pattern for wellness. Perhaps they have called the elders of the church for prayer and healing. They've sought out numerous physicians and other health professionals. They have received some form of treatment, tests, surgery, and more. They're told to rest, and in time, they will be well.

But not everyone's prescribed pattern turns out that way. In spite of all, disease hangs on; spirits dampen; hope can grow dim very quickly.

Because of medical advances, we now *live* with illnesses more than we *die* from them. There are an estimated 55 million Americans who are chronically ill. There are many more millions with an illness that is short-term. And there are probably countless undershepherds giving care to those who are ill. Affliction makes a dent as well with pastors, counselors, friends, co-workers, and family members, even if they aren't undershepherds. And with the epidemic of new and strange diseases of the 80s and 90s, infirmity will only worsen. We must learn how to cope with this unwelcome visitor that, for some, never goes away. Affliction strikes the health-minded jogger as well as the couch potato; it is no respecter of persons.

Pain in this life is inevitable. Misery, however, is optional.

Every nightmare has a beginning, and mine started in 1979. Some would call it the "dark night of the soul." I call it chronic illness. I entered full-time Christian ministry in the field of Jewish evangelism in 1975. I traveled nearly full-time, speaking, and authored seven books in five years. I pushed too hard, slept too little, ate the wrong things, and didn't know what a vacation was. A weekend off occurred when I spoke at one Sunday church service instead of two. Airports and lonely country roads were constant companions. But I figured that in my line of work the laborers truly were few, so I should work twice as hard to fill in all the gaps. Noble thought, but not a healthy one.

In the spring of 1979 I was besieged with a nameless disease that racked my body with exhaustion, flu-like body aches, mental confusion, low-grade fever, and more. The dilemma worsened each week. In the summer of 1979, I spent three days languishing in a Sioux Falls, South Dakota motel room, unable to fulfill any of the meetings in churches and women's groups that had been scheduled. I simply could not get out of bed due to exhaustion and the accompanying sleep loss.

My illness went undiagnosed and then misdiagnosed for nearly a decade. A dozen doctors insisted it was depression, but I knew I loved life and ministry too much to be labeled with depression alone. Between 1979 and 1987 I visited dozens of doctors and other health professionals. There were numerous hospitalizations, hundreds of lab tests, drug experimentation, and two dozen needless electric shock treatments. There was a lot of needless running around for answers, and when I did not fit my doctor's prescribed pattern of recovery, without exception he or she grew weary of my weariness and referred me elsewhere. It was a treadmill of horror. The only treatment that brought an ounce of relief was rest. But rest for a Type-A person is almost a four-letter word.

In 1985 the exhaustion and other symptoms forced me to step down from public ministry. I felt devastated and even abandoned by the God whom I was serving in full-time ministry. Being single and living alone, I spent relentless hours in isolation, pondering what went wrong. Was there some secret sin? Was repentance in order and, if so, repentance from what? Nothing made sense. I had led hundreds of people to the Lord and I had a wealth of teaching material that Christians needed to hear. Did God *send* this affliction? Far more likely the enemy did, but why did God allow it?

Apparently God wanted me quiet, giving him my full attention. That's tough to do when one works 60 to 70 hours a week. Two things were clear: there is no way that overwork can be sanctified, and no worker in Christian ministry is indispensable.

In 1987 while watching a local television talk show in Minneapolis, I learned of a new syndrome called the chronic Epstein-Barr virus. It would later be named the chronic fatigue syndrome (CFS) and also the chronic fatigue immune deficiency syndrome (CFIDS). It is believed to be a virus that takes over the body if one has a weakened immune system. And stress more than anything else weakens that immune system. The likelihood of this virus spreading to epidemic proportions is feared.

Shortly after that television program, I was diagnosed as having CFS. It is untreatable except by rest. For victims of this and many other diseases, there is a terrible grief process. I had gone to bed and stayed there in 1985. Depression and discouragement can be devastating, for the victim has lost his or her ministry/career, finances, friends who wouldn't "hang in there," self-esteem, purpose, and much more.

But at last I had a legitimate disease. This means more than the healthy world can know! I felt validated. It confirmed that I was neither lazy nor crazy, and that my condition was not all in my head as so many health professionals had suggested. I was not just a middle-aged woman at the mercy of my hormonal system. I had a virus—a virus that doesn't kill its victims though some wish it would. If exhaustion *could* kill, CFS victims would succumb in great numbers. Basically, it falls into a giant category of diseases that let one neither live nor die. Victims of such diseases truly begin to fear life far more than death.

While the meditations and prayers in this book will look at the "silence of God" in times of great trouble, they are not intended to be a vehicle of anger at God, nor at friends and loved ones who simply do not understand our situation. But this book will *not* encourage afflicted readers to deny the pain, to force a smile though the heart is breaking, to confess we are well when we're not, or to relax because God will turn our scars into stars (which he may very well do).

Infirmity hurts. Somehow short- or long-term illness will alter the course of uncounted numbers of people. It affects the afflicted, the undershepherds, and anyone who comes into contact with the afflicted person. No one is immune. I trust this book will be a window into the world of those who suffer in a body that has gone out of control. Victims need to be loved back to life, not abandoned or lectured with unwelcome advice.

Somehow, afflicted Christians, through the grace of God, must believe that something good will come from the ordeal, for God's economy wastes nothing! Great is the number of believers who have gone before us into the furnace of infirmity and who have come back and reported that God is still there in the midst of the pain.

Those of you who are well, will you bring comfort to the afflicted? Will you hold us up and have faith and hope for us when ours wears thin? Will you even reach out to unbelievers who are ill? Infirmity has converted many atheists and doubters, and has been known to turn lukewarm Christians into mighty warriors for God's kingdom.

Affliction transforms lives—either for good and for God, or for devastation and tragedy.

As Philip Yancey reminds us in his book, *Where Is God When It Hurts?*, "God is speaking to us through pain. . . . He can use it to make us aware of Him. The symphony He is working out includes minor chords, dissonance, and tiring fugal passages. But those of us who follow His conducting through these early movements will, with renewed strength, someday burst into song."

That song, if not on earth then in heaven, will contain no more illness, moody doctors, prescription drugs, painful surgeries, or family and friends who just don't understand.

Because Jesus is our blessed hope, the ultimate prognosis for these mortal bodies is perfection!

I owe more to the fire, hammer and chisel than to anything else in my Lord's workshop.

—C. H. Spurgeon

I can't believe that God "sends" illness to a specific person . . . a God who has a weekly quota of malignant tumors to distribute and consults His computer to find out who deserves one or who could handle it best.

—Rabbi Harold Kushner

Although the world is full of suffering, it is also full of people overcoming it.

—Helen Keller

Shattered Dreams

Illness is not bashful. It shows itself in spite of our best efforts. It generally saps our energy, makes us irritable, rearranges our lives, limits our social life, strains our relationships, clouds our plans for the future, and occupies our thoughts. Only God's grace and the love of our undershepherds allow us to hang in there on the merry-go-round of discomfort, doctor's appointments, drugs, tests, frustration, fears, and tears. Being sick is a major part of who we are. It can be a full-time job, for it goes wherever we go.

23

It is easy to feel imprisoned for a crime we didn't commit.

We almost forget what or who we were when we were well. Affliction dictates our emotions and actions —even facial expression and tone of voice. Our personality tends to be a mirrorlike reflection of the emotion we are struggling with at the time. There is often little strength left over to try to mask the emotions.

Well people have a sort of buffer zone that allows them to downplay life's annoyances. It would seem that affliction causes us to lose that ability and possibly even recoil in the other direction.

Yes, affliction shatters dreams, but God wants to build something new on the foundation of a broken heart or life. We must believe that God *will* give us something greater, and that he "will repay . . . for the years the locusts have eaten" (Joel 2:25). The greater the despair, the greater the Lord will prove to be.

But God seldom gives us a long-range view of the journey! We generally see the next stretch perhaps, and maybe that is the best way for us to practice faith. Oh how we wonder what lies ahead—but we can only take a step. And in faith we must believe God will show us the next step and dispense more grace. One day we will realize that he has led us to a glorious goal according to his wise plan. On some days it is difficult—and even incomprehensible—to believe that the hand of God is guiding us to that goal; yet that is the essence of faith and trust. We must learn from the heroes of faith in Hebrews 11. Hear them relate their experiences, tell of the darkness of their night, and disclose some of the humanly impossible situations in which they so often found themselves.

The burden may seem as gigantic as a mountain, but God has already figured out a way for us to climb it, and it begins with small steps. The peak that is nearest the storm clouds is also nearest the stars of light. God's mountain climbers—particularly those of us burdened with affliction—walk in precarious places. Yet, "He will make my feet like hinds' feet, and he will make me to walk upon [the] high places" (Hab. 3:19 KJV).

Shattered Dreams Hurt, Lord

Lord, my dreams have turned to dust.
My hopes and aspirations have turned to ashes.
The road map to my life has hit a dead end.
You're the only One who can
    restore order to the confusion,
    direction to the wandering,
    and purpose out of despondency.
Shattered dreams hurt, Lord.
They take years to build,
And only seconds to topple.
And now I'm back to zero.

But maybe that is where I need to be,
In order to be pliable in Your hands.
To have nothing on earth to which I cling,

To abandon all the security blankets,
  and
    to
      let
        go
          into the safety net
            You have provided for me!
So I'll give You back the dreams, Lord,
  though I may put up a fight.
But take them
  and reshuffle my priorities,
  aspirations
  and longings of the heart,
    and make them in perfect accord
    with Your plan for my life.

        Amen.

For Further Meditation

> Those who trust in the LORD are like Mount Zion, which cannot be shaken but endures forever. As the mountains surround Jerusalem, so the LORD surrounds his people both now and forevermore (Ps. 125:1–2).

> Even youths grow tired and weary, and young men stumble and fall; but those who hope in the LORD will renew their strength. They will soar on wings like eagles; they will run and not grow weary, they will walk and not be faint (Isa. 40:30–31).

> Forget the former things; do not dwell on the past. See, I am doing a new thing! Now it springs up; do you not perceive it? I am making a way in the desert and streams in the wasteland (Isa. 43:18–19).

> For I know the plans I have for you, declares the LORD, plans to prosper you and not to harm you, plans to give you hope and a future (Jer. 29:11).

> To him who overcomes, I will give the right to sit with me on my throne, just as I overcame and sat down with my Father on his throne (Rev. 3:21).

The promises of God are certain, but they do not all mature in 90 days.

—A. J. Gordon

With affliction, the past and the present must never be a measure of the future.

—author unknown

2

A Diagnosis: A New Chapter in Life

It is not unusual today to have an undefined illness or nameless disease. This can be as frustrating as the affliction itself. We need that official diagnosis so we are not grasping at straws, trying hit and miss tactics, wasting more money, time, and energy.

Receiving a diagnosis can temporarily look like a gift. The guesswork is over. In a sense, we've been vindicated. Our symptoms are justified and the situation is not "all in our head." We can't always pronounce our diagnosis; nonetheless, it is official and we are no longer in that nebulous netherworld where we are neither sick nor well. Yes, to us pain is pain, but we have a tough time convincing many people of that. And not only do friends and loved ones not take us seriously, without a diagnosis we have our own doubts and questions.

But with a diagnosis our credibility is, in a sense, restored! And there is more hope for a cure or treatment for now we are dealing with more certainties. We have relief from that nameless torment. Perhaps now we'll follow a pattern and the future won't be quite so cloudy. We'll know more what to expect, and we'll become familiar with methods that have helped others with the same affliction.

And, no, we weren't just seeking attention with our behavior before our diagnosis. We had a reason to seek financial aid. There was justifiable reason why we declined many social invitations and chose to retire at night about the time others were just going out. And there was a reason for our being irritable, impatient, and overly sensitive. Now we have a legitimate illness.

Now come a flood of questions: Will my life be drastically altered? Will I deteriorate and be unable to care for myself? Will loved ones abandon me? How will I support myself? How much physical and emotional pain will there be, and, can I handle it?

With a diagnosis we now know what we're fighting and we can somehow get on with life, even though our lives have been altered. A new climate of hope settles in—sort of a new beginning. We have entered a new chapter of life; it is not the end of normal life, but rather the end of not knowing what was wrong.

God can solve any mystery. He does not want us to grope in the dark forever, so his wisdom has permeated those who are treating us. The delay in revealing the cause of our affliction is not a statement that we will *never* know it. The delay may be God's way of asking us if we are willing to love and trust him even without all the answers.

I'm Weary Today, Lord

I'm weary today, Lord,
  of verbal games with peers,
  of breaking my back to be accepted,
  of trying to meet all my deadlines,
  of the routine
  of the rat race
  and most of all,
  of the spiritual valleys
    into
      which
        I
          plunge.

Forgive me, Lord,
  for self-centered introspection,
  for being insensitive to others,
  for making demands,
  for thinking I am so special,
  with unusual needs and rights,
  and a title claim to the good things in life.

Help me, Lord,
    to see Your handiwork in my failure,
    to exalt You in the midst of distress,
    to leap for joy when someone excels me,
    to have a quiet spirit when I am overlooked,
    to smile even if I'm misunderstood,
    to be joyful though my mind and body ache,
    to love when I feel the most unloved.

             Amen.

For Further Meditation

Have I not commanded you? Be strong and courageous. Do not be terrified; do not be discouraged, for the LORD your God will be with you wherever you go (Josh. 1:9).

Why are you downcast, O my soul? Why so disturbed within me? Put your hope in God, for I will yet praise him, my Savior and my God (Ps. 42:11).

I lift up my eyes to the hills—where does my help come from? My help comes from the LORD, the Maker of heaven and earth. He will not let your foot slip—he who watches over you will not slumber; indeed, he who watches over Israel will neither slumber nor sleep (Ps. 121:1–4).

He gives strength to the weary and increases the power of the weak (Isa. 40:29).

This is what the LORD says: "In the time of my favor I will answer you, and in the day of salvation I will help you; I will keep you" (Isa. 49:8).

Suffering will either be your master or your servant, depending on how you handle the crises of life. A crisis doesn't make a person — it reveals what a person is made of.

—Warren Wiersbe

For if our suffering weighs heavy, so does the blessing it contains.

—Basilea Schlinck

In Training
for Reigning

At one time we were well. Few of us can look at a calendar and point to the day we became ill. The process generally sneaks up gradually, altering life in subtle ways. But what may have started out as an irritation, slowly takes over our lives. Something has gone terribly wrong.

Those of us with invisible illnesses appear healthy. We don't have scars, bandages, crutches, or a wheelchair. Nonetheless there is pain that in some cases no doctor's probing fingers can define. Oftentimes no drug or treatment erases the problem.

35

There's also weakness and exhaustion. It's usually a profound fatigue—so much so that we feel like the Greek god Atlas holding up the world. We are nearly crushed beneath it, for the mental, emotional, and spiritual drain of an illness is all-consuming. And it is not unusual to awaken in the morning feeling just as fatigued as when we fitfully fell asleep. For many, escape comes only in minute snatches of restless sleep.

We never thought when we first noticed some strange symptoms and malaise that illness would take over our lives. It never entered our minds that for some this cycle of illness would one day become a normal condition, also known as chronic illness. And in this age of high technology and medical break-throughs, we certainly didn't expect to spend months, years, or a lifetime with a malady for which there is no known treatment.

We are fighting a microscopic war. The size of the enemy may barely be visible under a microscope, yet it completely drains us.

Nobody plans on being consumed by infirmity. We go through life dodging all sorts of foes, but we never expected this.

Paul Billheimer in his classic book, *Don't Waste Your Sorrows*, contends that in God's economy, all affliction is intended to drive us to God. Billheimer puts forth some biblically sound concepts that suggest we are in training for reigning, for in 2 Timothy 2:12 (KJV) it says, "If we suffer, we shall also reign with him." This is expressed elsewhere in Scripture on several occasions. It is the theology that says those who suffer constitute the princes of the ethereal realm.

Could we be wasting what God intended for our growth? In our insistence on being totally well, could we be wasting an enhanced rank in eternity? Could we even be wasting some earthly assignment? God can most effectively use those who have been broken—broken in wealth, self-will, ideals, reputation, ambitions, health, and much more.

All believers experience the refiner's fire, and affliction is an all-consuming holocaust. But God's hand is on the thermostat. He truly does know how much we can take. Regrettably, the distorted lenses we wear because of affliction cause us to lose sight of that perspective.

Abundant Living

You're a miracle worker, Lord,
  and I'm in need of one.
You don't have to part the sea for me,
  or send manna from heaven,
  but a small-scale miracle
  would restore my faith
  and see me through another week
  crowded with
    decisions
    disappointments
    doubts
    deadlines
    and dilemmas.
A week perhaps light on the victories.
A week not promising the abundant life.

But, Father, You came that we might
   have an abundant life.
   You came to offer peace,
   even when life lies shattered at our feet
   in a million little pieces.

Perhaps I've been too caught up in a miracle;
Too caught up with needing a sign.
Perhaps all I really need to do
   is appropriate all of Your marvelous promises!

Amen.

For Further Meditation

So do not fear, for I am with you; do not be dismayed, for I am your God. I will strengthen you and help you; I will uphold you with my righteous right hand (Isa. 41:10).

When you pass through the waters, I will be with you; and when you pass through the rivers, they will not sweep over you. When you walk through the fire, you will not be burned; the flames will not set you ablaze (Isa. 43:2).

The LORD your God is with you, he is mighty to save. He will take great delight in you, he will quiet you with his love, he will rejoice over you with singing (Zeph. 3:17).

In this you greatly rejoice, though now for a little while you may have had to suffer grief in all kinds of trials. These have come so that your faith—of greater worth than gold, which perishes even though refined by fire—may be proved genuine and may result in praise, glory and honor when Jesus Christ is revealed (1 Peter 1:6–7).

What the world needs is an amplifier for the still, small voice.

—author unknown

I believe in the sun even when it is not shining; I believe in love even when I feel it not; I believe in God, even when He is silent.

—found on a concentration camp wall

4

Hearing
the Silence of God

Desperate people try desperate measures. Afflicted people are prone to try just about anything for relief. We change our diets, our lifestyles, our exercise programs, our friends, and our jobs if too stressful. We earnestly seek prayer for healing. We visit countless doctors and other health professionals. We try medications, surgeries, vitamins, supplements, and more. If we had a dollar for every new herbal tea rage, mushroom therapy, or ancient Chinese remedy that is tossed our way, we would at least be wealthy in our infirmity! We join support groups for encouragement. Some Christians even venture into dangerous territory, and, out of desperation, experiment in healing techniques that are occult-oriented.

We feel stretched in many directions at once. We struggle to surrender and accept, then decide to keep forging ahead and fight. There seems to be a fine line between giving up and giving in. And we are often caught looking skyward with pained, anxious faces, as if to say, "You say God cares for me? Perhaps I can take better care of myself." After all, we're doing all we know how to do to get well. What does God have to say? Why is he silent?

How we strain to hear just a word from God in the midst of our dilemma. If we could put on a set of amplifiers, maybe we could hear him. Just one word— a word that will help us believe that someday things will be all right again. That our world won't *stay* shattered, and even if it does, God will take care of all the details, fears, apprehensions, and unknown factors. Just a whisper from him? There seems to be none.

A word is *always* on the way, though it may not arrive at just the time we had hoped. For there is a fullness of time when things do happen. Just as "in the fullness of time God sent forth his Son," so time always flows toward fullness and purpose. He is at work when the diagnosis comes back saying, "there's nothing more we can do." He is at work when a prescription for pain medication must be increased. He is at work when we are told our condition is untreatable and incurable. For God runs *ahead* of our prayers!

Job became disillusioned with God and couldn't praise him. He could only lament, and he was insistent in his desire to break the hiddenness and silence of God. He longed to address God face to face. This longing is a natural human reaction.

Sick people are the first ones to doubt God's love.

It is foolish to be told to contain our "whys." They are a part of being human. But the "whys" don't have to be hurled at God. They can be asked with reverence, in prayer.

Fine-tune Our Hearing, Lord

Such a paradox it seems, that man,
With all his electronic hearing devices . . .
   the amplifiers
   the earphones
   the stereophonic and quadraphonic sound,
Is still so very deaf
   To the cry of humanity in need.
Deaf to the pleas to be understood
   or loved
   or appreciated.
Yes, deaf even to God,
Who doesn't speak with flashing neon lights
Or electronic megaphones,
But rather communicates through
That still, small voice,
That requires us only to be still,
To be very quiet,
And to listen.

And maybe, if we listen so carefully,
We will have the most meaningful dialogue
We have yet to experience.

Fine-tune our hearing, Lord.
My generation won't make it
Unless we hear from You.

Amen.

For Further Meditation

This is what the LORD, the God of your father David, says: "I have heard your prayer and seen your tears; I will heal you" (2 Kings 20:5).

The righteous cry out, and the LORD hears them; he delivers them from all their troubles (Ps. 34:17).

"For my thoughts are not your thoughts, neither are your ways my ways," declares the LORD. "As the heavens are higher than the earth, so are my ways higher than your ways and my thoughts than your thoughts" (Isa. 55:8–9).

Praise be to the God and Father of our Lord Jesus Christ, the Father of compassion and the God of all comfort, who comforts us in all our troubles, so that we can comfort those in any trouble with the comfort we ourselves have received from God. For just as the sufferings of Christ flow over into our lives, so also through Christ our comfort overflows (2 Cor. 1:3–5).

A friend is a person with whom I may be sincere. Before him, I may think aloud.

—R. W. Emerson

A good friend will joyfully sing with you when you are on the mountaintop, and silently walk beside you through the valley.

—author unknown

Remember, everyone you meet is fighting a battle.

—author unknown

5

Loneliness Hurts

Affliction produces loneliness. The absence of those who love us does not mean they don't care, however; they are caught up in their own cares as well. How we long so often to share our innermost feelings with even one who might understand. Some support groups are effective, but the chronically ill or seriously ill often cannot make the journey.

When an illness is raging, when pain is rampant, when the future looks dim for us, we long to pour out our hearts to someone. Just *one* person would do. We probably couldn't handle an army of exhorters!

But often we rest in solitude. Fear grips us. Doubt creeps in and perhaps a sense of hopelessness. If confined or left alone for too long, we can easily give in and give up.

Friends and loved ones certainly care, but all too often, even in their willingness to lift us up, they may want to talk about matters that mean little to those of us who hurt. They mean well; it's just that they have not walked in our shoes.

Loneliness devastates us and slows our recovery. Our thought processes become muddled and distorted when we can't fully share our feelings. We start to dwell on the negative and lose sight of hope.

At this point we simply must reach out. We should not be ashamed to call a friend or a loved one and express our feelings; we may even ask them, in spite of their busy schedules, if they would talk on the telephone for a while or pay us a visit. We may even have to ask them to listen, for they may be preoccupied with other things. The world of the well is in a time capsule set at fast-forward. Though they care about us, they also must deal with their own stresses, problems, and disappointments.

We must not hesitate to state frankly: "I am hurting and I need to talk. Just a few minutes. Would you help me sort out my thoughts and anxieties? Would you pray with me? Would you take just a moment and help by loving me back to life?"

With our expectations in line, just a brief visit can lift us immeasurably! But we must recognize that often we simply have to ask for help.

We as afflicted people must learn to risk, to reach out, to ask for help when needed. We fear being a burden. Talking to God and knowing that he is listening and caring is vital. But our humanity stares us in the face as well. We were designed to have loving people around us and should not feel guilty for this desire. We must also be careful not to put more confidence in people than in God.

God can heal us instantly. Expressions of love from others—a listening ear, a caring heart—can heal as well, though the healing may take much longer. People are not a *replacement* for God, but they certainly can be his instruments on this earth.

Nobody Else Will Listen, Lord

I had a monumental need today, Lord.
I needed someone to talk to.
I needed a conversation that went beyond
   my neighbor's rose bushes, or
   last night's election results.
Such a paradox it seems,
   to be surrounded by people,
   to have their voices vibrating through me,
   to be numb from shaking hands,
   to hurt from smiling . . .
   and yet to feel alone.
Alone because conversations
   center on things of insignificance for eternity.
Because conversations focus on
   the high cost of living
   and not on the Giver of life.

Yes, alone in a crowd,
But never alone, Lord,
   for You listen
   even if I ramble and make little sense,
   or if I can't quite explain myself,
   or if I am redundant
   and never get to the point.
Thank You, Father,
   for being my Companion,
        Confidant,
        and Counselor,
And for listening, when all the world
Is caught up with the fun and games of life,
Too busy with yesterday's sports results
To listen to a needy soul.

                    Amen.

For Further Meditation

> I love you, O LORD, my strength. The LORD is my
> rock, my fortress and my deliverer; my God is
> my rock, in whom I take refuge. He is my shield
> and the horn of my salvation, my stronghold. I
> call to the LORD, who is worthy of praise, and I
> am saved from my enemies (Ps. 18:1–3).

> Turn to me and be gracious to me, for I am
> lonely and afflicted (Ps. 25:16).

> Then you will call, and the LORD will answer;
> you will cry for help, and he will say: Here am I
> (Isa. 58:9a).

> I was sick and you looked after me . . . I tell you
> the truth, whatever you did for one of the least
> of these brothers of mine, you did for me (Matt.
> 25:36–40).

> I will not leave you as orphans; I will come to
> you (John 14:18).

He who laughs . . . lasts.

—Tim Hansel

Blessed is he who has learned to laugh at himself, for he shall never cease to be entertained.

—John Powell

6

Laughter:
The Best Medicine

There are days when laughter can only spring up within us as a gift from God. Our pain, disappointment, inconvenient lifestyle, and frustration would like to forever extinguish the spark of laughter that, if ignited, could cause a wave of healing joy throughout our body. It is a scientific fact that laughter releases endorphins in the brain—the body's natural relaxant and antidepressant. It is also a fact that negative feelings can produce sickness, so it is true that joy and laughter and love produce positive chemical reactions in the body.

If we are always serious, there will be no respite from our infirmity. We must try, with every ounce of strength we have, to find the positive and the humorous despite the seriousness of our ordeal.

Laughter helps us put things into a better perspective. Somehow it offers hope. It costs us nothing, and it lightens the cares and worries of the day. Everything is easier to bear. Laughter is a natural Valium, and it takes far fewer muscles to laugh than to cry. Yes, we can laugh—even at ourselves! With God's grace, the joy of the Lord can be tapped into!

At the same time, it is important to choose undershepherds who have the gift of humor. Undershepherds who have such a gift can create laughter in the most delicate situations. No, not loud, boisterous, ill-timed, or inappropriate humor; rather, the ability to see in every situation an appropriate brand of joy. And that joy and laughter is contagious. It's the *only* contagious commodity we can hope to be infected by! No matter how devastating the short- or long-term illness may be, we will feel healthier, more alive, and more hopeful if laughter is in our midst.

Laughter and humor may be worth a thousand prescription medications!

An anonymous poet penned the following:

> Are you worsted in a fight?
> Are you cheated of your right?
>> Laugh it off.
> Don't make tragedies of trifles,
> Don't shoot butterflies with rifles —
>> Laugh it off.
> Does your work get into kinks?
> Are you near all sorts of brinks?
>> Laugh it off.
> If it's sanity you're after,
> There's no recipe like laughter,
>> Laugh it off.

The poem may lack theological sophistication, but its message is right on. Laughter is a medication with no side effects, and it's one form of addiction we must have.

Endurance Test

I know You have a sense of humor, Lord,
But are You laughing at me?
I have so many skinned knees and black and blue
    marks
From the game of life.
I'm a walking target, Lord,
    numb from the darts being tossed at me,
    weary from not being understood,
    heavy laden from having my motives
    questioned,
    heartbroken as an unbelieving world
    cheers me on
    to make a bigger fool of myself.

Father, help me not to take myself so seriously;
Not to strive for perfection,
   or the highest score,
   or the most expensive look,
   or the best sales record.
Help me to be content to be worthy in Your eyes
   alone.

             Amen.

For Further Meditation

> You have filled my heart with greater joy (Ps. 4:7).

> Weeping may remain for a night, but rejoicing comes in the morning (Ps. 30:5).

> Let me hear joy and gladness; let the bones you have crushed rejoice (Ps. 51:8).

> A happy heart makes the face cheerful, but heartache crushes the spirit (Prov. 15:13).

> A cheerful heart is good medicine (Prov. 17:22).

> For our light and momentary troubles are achieving for us an eternal glory that outweighs them all (2 Cor. 4:17).

All human wisdom is summed up in two words: wait and hope.

—Alexandre Dumas

The word hope I take for faith; indeed hope is nothing else but the constancy of faith.

—John Calvin

7

Waiting Tests Faith

Sickness turns our lives into a waiting game. Early stages of affliction are particularly difficult as we wait for test results, for a diagnosis, and for a pattern to our dilemma. Then we wait for medication to take effect, or for a cure, or at least for a medical breakthrough. We wait for the illness to just run its course. And we wait for answered prayer to bring us the miracle we often need.

We become rather adept at waiting and hoping, although not naturally. It takes work to let faith and hope be in charge. It takes blood, sweat, and tears; it takes failure and starting over again. Humanity in general is lousy at waiting.

Though waiting is a tough assignment, the ability for us to hold steady will give God unlimited sway. Waiting is a great part of life's discipline and God frequently exercises the grace of waiting in those who are anxious and hurried.

Waiting—often waiting until problems have reached a climax—has always been a plan of God. Jesus worked this way with his disciples when they were in great distress during the storm at sea. God could have calmed the *first* wave but then the disciples would never have become acquainted with the power of Jesus. God often lets those waves rise high, as he did for the children of Israel at the crossing of the Red Sea, so his name can be magnified.

Waiting tests the patience of faith. It also allows time for preparation for the coming gift. It makes the blessing sweeter when it arrives. And it shows that God is sovereign—giving when and how he pleases.

Because of the desperation of our affliction, we tend to take everything into our own hands and we almost bind God's hands.

God leads us into the school of waiting. There he wants to give us so much that could be learned no other way: patience, humility, steadfast faith, and much more. God really wants to give us *more* than just the help we are asking, but he may first ask us to graduate from the school of waiting.

But remember, well people must go through this school as must afflicted people. Our courses may be a bit different, but *every one* of us lives in the world of waiting—waiting for God to choose when and how he will act.

It's One of Those Days, Lord

It's one of those days, Lord,
When life isn't full of warm feelings,
And serenity seems as elusive as a May
    butterfly.
Reality is stabbing at me unmercifully,
Causing me to want to seek refuge in a world of
    fantasy.
My mind is muddled, Lord.
I can't even articulately communicate with You.
I take comfort in knowing that You interpret
The innermost longings and pleadings of my
    heart.
Perhaps You are shaking me up;
I'm reminded that You not only comfort the
    afflicted,
But that You also afflict the comfortable.
And, yes, I've been mired in complacency of late.
My responsiveness to You has been pitifully
    weak,

Unless I've had a
   special conflict
   heavy decision
   recurring problem
   or annoying relationship.
Too often, Lord, I treat Your promises
As carelessly
As those Salvation Army clothes I discarded.
I never gave them another thought.
Thank You for sifting through muddled
   thoughts, Lord,
And through well-worn clichés,
   broken promises
   incoherent pleadings
   and halfhearted commitments.
Thank You for keeping communication lines
   open,
And for the assurance that I am never forsaken
Even when I tune You out
As easily as changing a channel.

            Amen.

For Further Meditation

Wait for the LORD; be strong and take heart (Ps. 27:14).

Wait for the LORD and he will exalt you (Ps. 37:34).

I wait for the LORD, my soul waits, and in his word I put my hope (Ps. 130:5).

It is good to wait quietly for the salvation of the LORD (Lam. 3:26).

Then Jesus told him, "Because you have seen me, you have believed; blessed are those who have not seen and yet have believed" (John 20:29).

Now faith is being sure of what we hope for and certain of what we do not see (Heb. 11:1).

My God, I have never thanked you for my thorn. I have thanked you for my roses, but not once for my thorn. . . . Those miserable, prickly thorns! What eternal weights of glory they may be.

—George Matteson

8

God's Servant Job:
Lessons from an Ash Heap

Most of us with a serious short- or long-term illness have wondered if we are some twentieth-century manifestation of Job. One of Job's many problems was infirmity. Who of us has not, in our fanciful imagination, seen ourselves sitting on an ash heap, if not covered with boils, then covered with surgical scars, bandages, or wounds inflicted by a doctor's probing instruments? Job's struggle seems overwhelming and so does ours. And, like Job, we want instant answers to our justifiable lament.

We can thank God for the Book of Job! He learned some lessons and spared us the pain of having to walk through them. Job addresses the needs of all humankind and touches the heart of every reader. He deals with the perplexities which torment everyone.

Job particularly anguished over the feeling that God did not care about him. But in fact, Job was special to God, and God called him "my servant" (Job 1:8). In his day, he was a "mover and a shaker" on behalf of the kingdom of God. And so it is today—our greatest teachers and leaders are often the greatest sufferers.

Job accused God of being indifferent and uncaring. He became a faultfinder of God and demanded an explanation. He truly shook a fist at God, and he reflects the turmoil of an honest heart.

When God spoke to Job "out of the whirlwind," he did little explaining or apologizing. Because he is God, he seeks no self-justification and he will not be patronizing.

God reminds all who suffer that we have limited understanding. He also instructs us through the Book of Job to take heart in the orderliness of nature when we begin to doubt God. If there is obvious order in the universe, we can conclude there is even more order and purpose in what we would call the chaos of our lives. God broods over everything he has made.

Perhaps the ultimate lesson in the Book of Job is that God's silence does *not* equate his absence. If we could only get into the mind-set that we can trust God when there seems a delayed response from him. Bigger plans are on the way, as with Job! Delay is just one of God's "filter systems" and his silence is a portion of his strategy.

As the scenario winds down, Job puts his hand on his mouth and is silenced as he sees the face of God. Job is an eloquent speaker, but in the presence of God, he is speechless. Now God and Job could move on to a new level of fellowship and communion.

God hears. He hears our groanings, our petitions, our prayers, our praise, our weeping. But to God, what happens *to* us is important and will determine what happens *through* us. Affliction truly reveals what we are made of, and affliction can become the laboratory for sincere spiritual discovery and growth.

Love Story

This morning I strayed, Lord.
Like an undirected sheep,
I thought I'd venture out on my own;
With the innocence and exuberance of a child,
I took off to do my own thing . . .
   to explore
   search for new horizons
   new opportunities
   adventures
And in my own self-sufficient way,
I left You in the dust
Without even an acknowledgment.
Tonight I'm asking that You take me back,
   unconditionally
   wholeheartedly
   and with no questions asked.

The miracle of our relationship
Is that You are waiting with open arms
   and forgiveness
   and gentleness
   and love
Before I even ask to be reinstated.

Father, thanks for not keeping score;
Or keeping track of my rebelliousness,
Or hitting me with a bad conduct report card.
Rather, You always take me back
No matter how far I stray.

               Amen.

For Further Meditation

You are my hiding place; you will protect me from trouble and surround me with songs of deliverance (Ps. 32:7).

God is our refuge and strength, an ever present help in trouble (Ps. 46:1).

Praise the LORD, O my soul, and forget not all his benefits. He forgives all my sins and heals all my diseases (Ps. 103:2–3).

Where can I go from your Spirit? Where can I flee from your presence? If I go up to the heavens, you are there; if I make my bed in the depths, you are there. If I rise on the wings of the dawn, if I settle on the far side of the sea, even there your hand will guide me, your right hand will hold me fast (Ps. 139:7–10).

Being confident of this, that he who began a good work in you will carry it on to completion until the day of Christ Jesus (Phil. 1:6).

Don't let tomorrow use too much of today.
—author unknown

God begs you to leave the future to Him while you mind the present.
—George MacDonald

9

A Day at a Time

"One day at a time" certainly has the ring of a cliché, and yet it is a mandatory philosophy with which the afflicted must come to terms. For now, long-range goals must be set aside. Even short-range plans must be put on the back burner, for our lives are temporarily on hold. Again the reality of illness underscores the limited power we have over our lives.

It's not easy to count the minutes, realizing that every day is a further postponement of the life we once knew. Friends and opportunities are passing us by while we're standing still. We are waiting to live, but we must do so in small bits of time.

But faith doesn't concern itself with the entire journey. One step at a time is enough. The first step is all that is needed, for "the LORD will guide you always" (Isa. 58:11).

Like toddlers we take a few small steps forward each day and try to relish the moments. By focusing on one day at a time, eventually we can look *back* and we are amazed at how far we've come on this bumpy road. No, it's certainly not the rat race speed of modern times that considers long-range nest eggs for retirement, or a new condo when the kids leave home. Rather, it's being content to deal with the immediate, and that is a foreign way of life to nearly everyone.

In fact, some must live *ten minutes* at a time, because the need for constant rest is a drama played out hourly, not just daily. But it's okay to take small steps—to read for ten minutes, then rest; to talk with a friend for ten minutes, then rest; to write for ten minutes, then rest. No, we won't set the world on fire with our accomplishments—but then we are the only ones really counting our accomplishments. God has asked us to be fully dependent on him for *every* moment of a twenty-four-hour day.

For those who are well, the days, weeks, and months rush by. For the afflicted, the clock and the calendar seem to stand still. Hope for tomorrow must be there, but the focus of attention must be on *today*. Yesterday is gone; tomorrow is not yet ours. Rather, *"This is the day the LORD has made; let us rejoice and be glad in it"* (Ps. 118:24).

Risk

Lord, I'm afraid I have a morbid preoccupation
With rejection and ridicule.
A feeling that I'm not measuring up,
And that my love will be refused.
I want to put the stage costume in mothballs
And be for real;
But it's too unsafe,
And I might not be in control of things.
Being genuine,
Not artificial,
Seems to me a threat.

Create in me a freedom, Lord,
To be real.
To have a childlike abandon
Of decades of chains.

To be willing to
   change
   alter direction or course
   accept another viewpoint
   accept my imperfections
   risk my innermost thoughts
   and look inward less
   and upon others more.

Lord, may I be secure enough in You
That I can stand up under any painful dart
That tells me I'm not being received
With a standing ovation.

                    Amen.

For Further Meditation

> On my bed I remember you; I think of you through the watches of the night. Because you are my help, I sing in the shadow of your wings. I stay close to you; your right hand upholds me (Ps. 63:6–8).

> Praise the LORD! Praise God in his sanctuary; praise him in his mighty firmament! Praise him for his mighty deeds; praise him according to his exceeding greatness! Let everything that breathes praise the LORD! (Ps. 150:1, 2, 6).

> For I am convinced that neither death nor life, neither angels nor demons, neither the present nor the future, nor any powers, neither height nor depth, nor anything else in all creation, will be able to separate us from the love of God (Rom. 8:38–39).

> Blessed is the man who perseveres under trial, because when he has stood the test, he will receive the crown of life that God has promised to those who love him (James 1:12).

All of us need a faith that will not shrink when washed in the waters of affliction and adversity.

—author unknown

A person's most fervent prayers are not said when he is on his knees, but when he is flat on his back.

—author unknown

10

Please Be Patient; I'm on Hold

For those of us who are production-minded and goal-oriented and who base a good self-image on accomplishments, it can be devastating to have to take pride in small achievements. When goals and purpose seem to leave us due to illness, inadequacy and a sense of failure move in unless we check them. With God's grace, we must let go of achievements, rewards, bonuses, applause, and even acclaim we may have had when well. Perhaps they were too important to us anyway.

Our life is, temporarily at least, different than it used to be, but it is not less significant. Identity is not based on achievements; our worth isn't tied in with our creativity or the fruit of our labor. How much better to be known by our investment in God and people than by profits or production.

So we focus on inner worth rather than external achievements. Our affliction is causing the development of a character that could never be attained in other ways. Ours is a school of training in patience, long-suffering, perseverance, empathy, faith, self-control, and more.

How we used to function in life doesn't matter now. What matters is that we learn to structure our lives, goals, and expectations around our present limitations, yet never give up hope that we will someday be our old selves again.

God *does* have a goal and a purpose for our lives, and that is to bring forth fruit. Our lives are not in vain even in infirmity. God comes to us as a vinedresser, pruning us. The more he prunes, the more fruit we will bear in future ministries. Though we may feel we are withering away and wasting time in our ordeal, we need to rejoice in the assurance that we are being prepared for greater fruitfulness!

Be Patient with Us, Lord

Lord, You must feel like washing Your
    hands of us some days.
Do You ever tire of
    shaking fists
    defiant rebellion
    indifference
    or being taken for granted?
Do You ever want to let our ship go down
    and let us pick up our own pieces?
Great God, how we need You!
Not just to salvage the wreckage,
But to rebuild broken spirits and bodies,
To remind us that You put it all together, once,

And that You still have the healing balm,
    to mend lives
    and spirits
    and bodies
    to give meaning to chaos
    purpose to the routine
    goals to the directionless
    order to the confusion
    love in spite of animosity
    and thanksgiving in spite of pain.
Be patient with us, Lord!
But remind us of our dependence and utter
    inability
To make it on our own.

                    Amen.

For Further Meditation

Yet you are enthroned as the Holy One; you are the praise of Israel. In you our fathers put their trust; they trusted and you delivered them. They cried to you and were saved; in you they trusted and were not disappointed (Ps. 22:3–5).

Ask and it will be given to you; seek and you will find; knock and the door will be opened to you. For everyone who asks receives; he who seeks finds; and to him who knocks, the door will be opened. . . . If you, then, though you are evil, know how to give good gifts to your children, how much more will your Father in heaven give good gifts to those who ask him (Matt. 7:7–8, 11).

Come unto me, all you who are weary and burdened, and I will give you rest. Take my yoke upon you and learn from me; for I am gentle and humble in heart, and you will find rest for your souls. For my yoke is easy and my burden is light (Matt. 11:28–30).

I have told you these things, so that in me you may have peace. In this world you will have trouble. But take heart! I have overcome the world (John 16:33).

When you can think of yesterday without regret and tomorrow without fear, you are near real contentment.

—author unknown

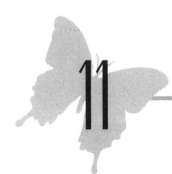

The Dilemma of Balance

Being ill is a full-time job without vacations or other fringe benefits. And it's a balancing act of the greatest magnitude! Balancing activity and anticipation with a daily routine of needed rest and quiet is not an easy assignment.

Balance is also needed in interpersonal relationships. We wonder if we should keep our dilemma private, or speak too often about it and risk the flight of loved ones. Should we ask for help and risk being a burden, or should we maintain some independence which can bring on isolation and other problems? Should we push ourselves socially in the interest of our mental health, or should we play it safe and virtually vegetate, thus allowing rest therapy a better chance of bringing recovery from our affliction?

Keeping a good balance thus involves a "pick and choose" mind-set. We must keep ourselves maintained for that is our *priority*. Everything else must be assigned a lower priority and some things just have to be let go for a time. Letting go is one of the most difficult assignments, for it is not just the *act* of letting go, but embracing the mind-set of acceptance at the same time.

Living among healthy people who have no restrictions offers us overwhelming temptation to depart from a strict recovery program that includes a needed balance. Well people will want us to make commitments, which can be a double-edged sword. With commitment there is anticipation; however, there is also the dread of not being able to follow through with that commitment. Then anticipation turns to stress, stress to anxiety, and anxiety to even poorer health.

Even good stress needs balance. Good stress is an event or opportunity that involves fun, activity, and people we love. It involves fellowship, caring, sharing, and love. But it also may involve too many people, too much talking, and too much activity. Then we're back to square one.

To arrive at a proper level of balance amidst affliction takes the help of Holy Spirit discernment. At the
start of each new day, we need to seek God's guidance
for the hours before us. We don't want to squander
them; rather, we should make every minute count,
not just for God, but for our recovery process.

Finding balance in an unbalanced world with the
complication of affliction can only be accomplished
by surrendering our day to the will of God. He will
redeem it and make it count, even if in our eyes it
seems but a wasteland. God does all things well, and
he specializes in turning ugliness into beauty and
wastelands into gardens.

Empathy

Oh, did I risk today, Lord.
I tiptoed into dangerous territory.
I closed my eyes and had to be pushed,
But in I went
And I'm here to tell You it wasn't easy!

I reached out to love, but no one accepted it.
They turned away, themselves unable to risk.
I reached out to share what I had
    and it was refused,
As people looked at me skeptically,
    questioning my motives.
I reached out to bear another's burden,
But they refused, for they could not confide in
    me.
I reached out to give myself away
But I nearly had to pay someone to accept me!

I can never risk again, Father!
It was too painful.
I think I'll duck back under my turtle shell
And let the hurting world go by me,
Giving little thought or care to it.
It's so much safer,
And besides, I'm such a wounded healer.
That is, Father, unless You empower me
To reach out and risk again,
      and again,
       and yet another time.
Come to think of it,
Very few wanted what You had to offer either.
I guess You know how I feel.

          Amen.

For Further Meditation

I will not die but live, and will proclaim what the LORD has done (Ps. 118:17).

He heals the brokenhearted and binds up their wounds (Ps. 147:3).

I am the LORD, the God of all mankind. Is anything too hard for me? (Jer. 32:27).

He took up our infirmities and carried our diseases (Matt. 8:17).

Dear friend, I pray that you may enjoy good health and that all may go well with you, even as your soul is getting along well (3 John 2).

He will wipe away every tear from their eyes. There will be no more death or mourning or crying or pain, for the old order of things has passed away. He who was seated on the throne said, "I am making everything new!" (Rev. 21:4–5).

Extraordinary afflictions are not always the punishment of extraordinary sins, but sometimes the trial of extraordinary grace. Sanctified afflictions are spiritual promotions.

—Matthew Henry

12

Why Me, Lord?

God can take it, but he shouldn't have to; that is, take our anger and general all around abuse because we're sick. In our perspective, God is not intervening; and so the quagmire of questions begins.

"Why me, Lord?" is the most popular. It suggests, however, that someone else might have been a better choice for this unjust round of suffering.

Then there is, "Have I done something terribly wrong? Have I committed some unpardonable sin, and if so, Lord, what is it?"

And then, "If God loves me as much as everyone says, why doesn't he ease my pain?"

Actually, the questioning and doubting are an endless winding road that leads nowhere. Even in heaven we may not be given answers to the questions of life and death and the drama lived out in between.

But Satan likes to torment us with suggestions that we're too sinful to be recipients of God's grace, mercy, and healing power. He nags at us that God can't totally be trusted, and that perhaps God is playing a "cat and mouse" game with us. If it looks like we're enjoying life too much, God leans over and hits us with a celestial club.

It's bad enough to be sick, to lose jobs, friends, and possibly our futures; now here's an additional nagging that God has separated himself from us. This can almost be the proverbial straw to break the camel's back.

Christian doctor Paul Brand was asked to comment on people's reaction to pain and suffering. He indicated that people hung up with the questions "Why me?" and "What did I do to deserve this?" often bitterly turned against God or else resigned themselves to a fatalistic despair. The most triumphant sufferers were those who sought the best response for a Christian and thus trusted God fully, despite their painful conditions.

While it is true that God never promised us a germ-free bubble in which to dwell, it's easy to think that because we're the "King's kids," our road will be smooth.

Yet someday we will probably learn that affliction has nothing to do with being right or wrong, or a good or a lukewarm Christian. The purpose of affliction is higher.

We are living on a stained planet; suffering, accidents, and other disasters are going to occur. There is no place we can go for a vacation from the abnormality of the universe, from the effects of the Fall on every area of life, and from the conflicts within and without that have occurred for millenniums.

But God would have us freely choose to love him, even when that choice involves pain, for we are committed to him and not to our feelings and rewards.

Candid Camera

Great God, You know me through and through!
I've tried at times to cover up and to pretend.
I've played games with myself
And I've fooled a lot of people.
For a day I even fooled myself.
But, Lord, You have seen the real me,
And yet You go on
   loving
   forgiving
   and picking up the pieces.
There's no place to which I can escape from You.
There's no place to hide.
You know my heart before it feels.
You know my words before they are sentences.

You know my motives
   prejudices
   manipulations
   and selfish goals.
You know the hurt behind my smile,
The jealousy behind the handshake,
And the bitterness behind the pat on the back.
It's all there in vivid, living color, Lord . . .
The candid camera to my soul.
And the wonder of wonders is that none of it
Sways Your love and care for me even one
   degree!
Thanks for hanging on to me, Lord,
Even on days when I want to break our contract.

Amen.

For Further Meditation

> Blessed is the man who trusts in the LORD, whose confidence is in him. He will be like a tree planted by the water that sends out its roots by the stream (Jer. 17:7–8).

> Heal me, O LORD, and I will be healed; save me and I will be saved, for you are the one I praise (Jer. 17:14).

> We know that suffering produces perseverance; perseverance, character; and character, hope. And hope does not disappoint us, because God has poured out his love into our hearts by the Holy Spirit, whom he has given us (Rom. 5:3–5).

> To keep me from becoming conceited because of these surpassingly great revelations, there was given me a thorn in my flesh, a messenger of Satan, to torment me. Three times I pleaded with the Lord to take it away from me. But he said to me, "My grace is sufficient for you, for my power is made perfect in weakness." Therefore I will boast all the more gladly about my weaknesses, so that Christ's power may rest on me. That is why, for Christ's sake, I delight in weaknesses, in insults, in hardships, in persecutions, in difficulties. For when I am weak, then I am strong (2 Cor. 12:7–10).

We are not alone. We belong to the largest company in all the world . . . the company of those who have known suffering. So long as we can sweeten another's pain, life is not in vain.

—Helen Keller

You cannot cure your sorrow by nursing it; you can cure it by nursing another's sorrow.

—George Matteson

Looking on the Needs of Others

Affliction makes us myopic and causes us to look only on *our* needs. Scripture warns us against that, stating, "Do nothing from selfishness or empty conceit, but with humility of mind let each of you regard one another as more important than himself; do not merely look out for your own personal interests, but also for the interests of others" (Phil. 2:3–4 NASB).

Sick people are *not* exempted from that exhortation! Although we may be suffering, we do not have the privilege of endless complaint or of selfish longings, expecting others to forget or set aside their problems and focus only on ours.

Time is the one commodity we have in excess, and some of it can be channeled to the needs of others. For friends, family members, and undershepherds, we can pray; we can also send them an encouraging note. We can express deep interest in them—in their jobs, ministries, families, and more. We can build them up, and tell them how much we cherish and appreciate them—for who they are and not for what they do for us. Like anything of value, people should never be taken for granted. We all have a corner of our heart that longs for some appreciation.

Friends, family members, and undershepherds often spend time listening to us. But no one is locked into that role, for with everyone there should be as much give-and-take as possible, to keep relationships in balance. So we can listen to others. We may find that to be the highlight of their day, for busy people with many responsibilities and deadlines can feel empty and lonely. Well people with whom they are dealing probably don't have time to listen to them. We can.

We were created to be channels, not reservoirs. Suffering can make us selfish or sacrificing.

Paul reminds us that God comforts us in our trials so that we can comfort those in pain with the comfort we have received (2 Cor. 1:4). Thus, those of us who have known affliction are going to be the hand-picked instruments of God to bring relief to another. God is preparing us to meet the deep needs of others by bringing us through the rough places first.

Purpose

Last week, Lord,
I asked You to show me a purpose
For occupying this earth.
This week You've allowed me to
   lift another's burden
   weep with a stumbling friend
   heal the wounds of a broken spirit
   say "I'm sorry" to a deserving soul
   send a card as encouragement to a friend
   say "I forgive you" to a hurting soul
   say "forgive me" to another
   say "thank you" a dozen times
   limit my expectations of others
   bury a grudge
   pray for someone's healing
   and say "I love you" to many who needed
   to hear.

Lord, forgive me for doubting even a moment,
That You would answer the fervent prayer of
mine,
To be an instrument of Your peace!

Amen.

For Further Meditation

> The LORD has heard my weeping. The LORD has heard my cry for mercy; the LORD accepts my prayer (Ps. 6:8–9).

> He who dwells in the shelter of the Most High will rest in the shadow of the Almighty (Ps. 91:1).

> You will keep in perfect peace him whose mind is steadfast, because he trusts in you (Isa. 26:3).

> Carry each other's burdens, and in this way you will fulfill the law of Christ (Gal. 6:2).

> And the Lord's servant must . . . be kind to everyone (2 Tim. 2:24).

> Clothe yourselves with humility toward one another, because, God opposes the proud but gives grace to the humble (1 Peter 5:5).

When the darkness of dismay comes, endure until it is over, because out of it will come that following of Jesus which is an unspeakable joy.

—Oswald Chambers

14

Unhealthy Expectations

Because of our physical and emotional limitations, it is easy to let our expectations get out of control. Expectations of friends, family members, undershepherds, doctors, pastors, children, and parents. We *expect* them to understand our circumstances, even if they have never experienced a health setback.

Not only will many not understand, some will even have skepticism on their faces. Because so many illnesses are invisible, we may look well. In fact, a common statement is, "You look so good, you must be well." That is usually not the case and comments like that, though well-meaning, tend to invalidate our ordeal and make us defensive. Then bitterness, resentment, and frustration build and we're headed for real trouble.

Today there are many new diseases. Some are unpronounceable and totally unfamiliar. Our actual response to the illness can appear to be out of proportion to objective physical findings. Observable symptoms may *never* convince *anyone* of the severity of our condition. And, if our symptoms are vague or changeable, people tend to dismiss our predicament as minor, when in fact, symptoms may be raging, causing us great discomfort.

When people doubt the severity or even the existence of our struggle, the overall pain and frustration is intensified many times over, and our syndrome only gets worse!

We know we're not creating a mountain out of a molehill. *We* know that we are not espousing hypochondriacal complaints for attention or sympathy. But there may be days when even God's appointed undershepherds may grow weary of our weariness and desire to have a break.

It seems only safe to put expectations in God alone. The psalmist expresses it well: "My soul finds rest in God *alone* . . . He *alone* is my rock and my salvation; he is my fortress; I will never be shaken. Find rest, O my soul, in God *alone;* my hope comes from him" (Ps. 62:1, 2, 5).

God is gracious in sending us undershepherds. But there is a danger when we attempt to get our satisfaction and expectation met by mere human beings who are flawed and prone to their own self-centeredness. Sometimes God will allow our earthly support system to disappoint us lest our dependence get misplaced.

Our soul, and our aching body, must find rest in God alone. God is then free to let his undershepherds do their part, knowing we are first looking to him and then to his earthly vessels who minister to us.

You're My Best Friend, Lord

You're my best friend, Lord.
With You I can risk everything.
I don't have to worry about not
    measuring up
    or fitting in
    or having the best clothes
    or saying all the right things.
With You, I don't fear
    having a confidence betrayed
    not being understood
    or having my motivations questioned.
Our conversations are meaningful, Lord,
For unlike everyone I know,
    You listen, listen and listen again.
You don't get upset if I do all the talking.
You aren't keeping score.

You give me Your full attention
And You don't wonder how to break away
Lest You miss Your next appointment.
I simply can't turn You away from me.
Now may I be a friend like that to someone?
Show me the person who needs a friend,
And let me be to them what You have been
   to me.

          Amen.

For Further Meditation

> You, O LORD, keep my lamp burning; my God
> turns my darkness into light (Ps. 18:28).

> Even though I walk through the valley of the
> shadow of death, I will fear no evil, for you are
> with me; your rod and your staff, they comfort
> me (Ps. 23:4).

> Be my rock of refuge, to which I can always go;
> give the command to save me, for you are my
> rock and my fortress (Ps. 71:3).

> I praise you because I am fearfully and won-
> derfully made; your works are wonderful, I
> know that full well (Ps. 139:14).

> I have fought the good fight, I have finished the
> race, I have kept the faith (2 Tim. 4:7).

> Let us fix our eyes on Jesus, the author and per-
> fecter of our faith, who for the joy set before him
> endured the cross, scorning its shame, and sat
> down at the right hand of the throne of God
> (Heb. 12:2).

The child of faith can give the assuring confession that "heavenly promises" are not idle dreams. There is no "perhaps." He rests upon Divine promise that cannot fail.

—Herbert Lockyer

God seems to exact a diploma from His grueling school of experience. Courses are: discipline, suffering, faith, tests, and self-examination.

—author unknown

Peace Amidst the Pieces

Even among those who are well, many are having trouble with peace these days. There is stress in the world, for it seems only corporate profits count. There is massive depersonalization to the point where most feel like a computer card number with no further identity. The future seems cloudy to everyone, not just those who are ill. Unless we plug into God's love and his promises, both sick *and* well will be swallowed up by the dog-eat-dog mind-set that grips our world.

Jehovah-Shalom means "the LORD is Peace" (Judg. 6:24). Peace has nothing to do with our circumstances. It is not something, but rather, someone. Jesus offers us his peace: "Peace I leave with you; my peace I give you" (John 14:27). A *peace amidst the pieces* kind of assurance.

With affliction, we watch the world of the well pass us by. Activity and production equal fulfillment, not rest and peace.

True peace is found only in the presence, favor, and love of God. The bottom line for everyone—even those running to and fro—is that our inner life is like a troubled sea, driven to and fro with perplexing doubts, fears, and anxiety.

Whether one is sick or well, true peace is found only in the presence, favor, and love of God. Stillness, peace, and rest are a tranquillity of soul that springs from faith in God's sovereignty. At times for the afflicted, reason may be confounded and faith staggered. A calm, serene, and confident faith comes from knowing and believing his lordship—no matter what our circumstances. As we appropriate God's power, love, and faithfulness, a blessed peace and an unexplainable feeling of satisfaction can become ours in spite of pain, in spite of a life put on hold by affliction.

We attain this peace by believing God's promises, frequenting his throne, and seeking his glory in all things. God who is our peace makes possible every blessing of peace for those who are at peace with him.

God's miraculous power to calm troubled waters extends to the spiritual realm and even reaches into the deepest pit of darkness and illness. Amidst all that would tend to disrupt us, agitate us, and cause us to lose hope, God's rest, peace, and love are available.

This kind of peace does not come naturally when the body or emotions are crippled with disease. But remembering almighty God as our portion, his eternal covenant as our stay, his precious promises as our security, his atonement, and his home as our final destination, it is possible to have a peace that the world cannot understand.

Peace Amidst the Pieces

Lord, too often we see You as an escape hatch.
The world is being absorbed and devoured by
   mass production
   competition
   assembly lines
   depersonalization
   and technical wonders.
The vast electronic wilderness
Is actually chiseling away, bit by bit,
Any ounce of personal identity.
We feel but a number
As computers dialogue with us.
And so we create
   games
   clubs
   pastimes
   organizations

projects
causes
crusades
Yet still feel empty.
Father, help us to cope rather than escape.
Create in us a desire to revolutionize through
    You,
Rather than be conformed to a strange set
    of dog-eat-dog principles.
Give us a sense of Divine purpose;
A purpose in a world going to pieces,
    lacking direction
    meaning
    goals
    and a reason to live.

                    Amen.

For Further Meditation

> Be at rest once more, O my soul, for the LORD has been good to you (Ps. 116:7).

> Great peace have they who love your law (Ps. 119:165).

> For he himself is our peace (Eph. 2:14).

> And the peace of God, which transcends all understanding, will guard your hearts and your minds in Christ Jesus (Phil. 4:7).

> For God was pleased to have all his fullness dwell in him, and through him to reconcile to himself all things, whether things on earth or things in heaven, by making peace through his blood, shed on the cross (Col. 1:20).

> Let the peace of Christ rule in your hearts, since as members of one body you were called to peace (Col. 3:15).

Fear breeds loneliness and conflict; loneliness and conflict breed fear. To heal the world, we must give people an answer to fear.... As long as we shrink back in fear, we will not experience release from despair.

—Paul Tournier

Fear motivates Satan the way faith motivates God.

—author unknown

Fear:
The Silent Stalker

Affliction can do terrible things to its victims. It quickly calls forth anxiety and fear. And sick people often have an abnormal way of thinking. That's when loved ones must step in and counter false thinking, particularly fear.

Fear can be spelled *terror, dread,* or *panic.* A poor prognosis, a relapse, and even new methods of treatment for a disease can all cause fear to rage out of control.

Much fear in affliction is based on potential loss—loss of lifestyle, financial security, friends, dignity, purpose, changes in appearance and personality. Some Christians feel they must have committed the unpardonable sin and that has brought this calamity on them. One thing is certain: fear will complicate and exacerbate our afflictions.

There is perhaps no greater-repeated exhortation in the Bible than to "fear not." Easier said than done sometimes. And Satan knows the overwhelming debilitation fear can cause. It's been said by some in the health field that fear is the major contributor to illness, particularly illnesses of the mind.

Fear can be countered by love: the love of God and the love of God with skin on—our undershepherds and other loved ones. Afflicted Christians have a hard time hearing "the word from the Lord" concerning just about anything—including the predicament of illness. Minds are often confused and frequently cause us to think irrationally. We don't have a buffer zone around us like the world of the well people. Without that buffer zone we face numerous challenges that we cannot hurdle. We may often need to talk about our fear and insecurity with a loved one.

Fear enters in when we realize that chronic illness may mean forever. The Christian consumed with affliction easily forgets that "forever" for the believer is subject to the hand of God in our lives. God uses scientists to come up with cures. God's sovereign hand of healing has touched many. But even if the illness is forever on the earth, then our real "forever" lies in eternity when these aching, mortal bodies will be perfect.

We need to guard what we think and say. Apprehension is normal, but dread and paralyzing anxiety are not appropriate because they will cause tremendous setbacks. Negative thinking *can* lead to self-fulfilling prophecies.

Fear is rampant in the twentieth-century, and it is *not* limited to afflicted people. Many are padlocked in their homes, fearing burglaries, gang warfare, violence, terrorism, economic disaster, financial loss, and more. Fear has become a way of life—and perhaps that is why the explosion of new plagues and diseases.

The Christian is often referred to as a sheep which has no natural ability for fighting off its enemies. Thus fear is one of the sheep's characteristics. Our Good Shepherd knows that fear is our inherent weakness as we face our arch adversary, the devil. So Jesus says, "Fear not, little flock." He wants faith to supplant fear. Fear is like the sand of the machinery of life; faith is like the oil (see Prov. 3).

No matter what the diagnosis or prognosis, we need to focus on God's restoring power. The unbelieving world cannot do that, and thus they sink into despair.

Help Us to Be Unafraid, Lord

What paradoxes we are, Lord.
Within each of us is such a need . . .
   to reveal and yet conceal.
A need to shout, "I hurt"
And yet communicate falsely,
   "I've everything under control."
A need to reach out, saying,
   "Share my life; I'm lonely,"
While communicating
   "I'm too busy to get involved with you."
A need to know You more intimately,
While communicating spiritual
   indifference and complacency.
Help us to be unafraid, Lord,
   of ourselves
   of each other
   of You.

Help us accept each other. . . .
In spite of ourselves.
To look up and not down in fear;
To look forward and forget the past,
To look out and not in.
And to be comforted that You
   have everything under control.

Amen.

For Further Meditation

Do not be afraid, for I am with you (Gen. 26:24).

Though an army besiege me, my heart will not fear; though war break out against me, even then will I be confident (Ps. 27:3).

I sought the LORD, and he answered me; he delivered me from all my fears (Ps. 34:4).

When I am afraid, I will trust in you. In God, whose word I praise, in God I trust; I will not be afraid. What can mortal man do to me? (Ps. 56:3–4).

You of little faith, why are you so afraid? (Matt. 8:26).

Don't be afraid; just believe (Luke 8:50).

*When looking around and looking inward
brings only despair, try looking up.*

—author unknown

*I have a rage to live, yet a longing to pass on
out of this endless nightmare.*

—author unknown

17

Hope or Despair:
It's Our Choice

Hope is the hallmark for the Christian. We don't have to be like Ezekiel's "dry bones" (Ezek. 37) whose hope has perished. Those dry bones didn't put their trust in God. Their hope was misplaced, but God in his mercy still allowed them (Israel) to come back to life. He offers the same to us.

Hope is the heart of every human being. It causes us to get up in the morning and helps us to keep on

119

keeping on. It allows us some optimism despite circumstances. And it allows us to dream of a future when things will be brighter. When afflicted people lose hope, it is not unusual for them to pass on. They lose their ability to fight back—in the physical *and* spiritual realm. "Hope deferred makes the heart sick" (Prov. 13:12). Without hope, we can become engulfed in depression, neurotic behavior, irritability, confused thinking, fear, anger, and much more.

The Bible tells us we are in a war. We are in a war of a spiritual nature, but many of us who are afflicted are also in a war within our own bodies. It would seem that our bodies have betrayed us. And without hope, the chronically ill must deal with the possibility of a lifetime of anguishing war. After a number of months or years, we may cry out in exhaustion and pain, "Lord, I can no longer fight the good fight."

When we lose hope or when our faith falters, it is not unreasonable for us to ask undershepherds or other loved ones to carry them for us.

The opposite of hope leads down a winding, dangerous road called unbelief. "Lord, help my unbelief." Thus Bible characters experienced times of hopelessness. But the neverending spiral of shaky hope can lead to a situation in which all we can do is hang on. Someone once said that the thirteenth commandment God gave Moses was "hangeth in there." Hang on to hope; to our sanity; to our undershepherds; and most of all, to the promises in the

Bible regarding hope that are true no matter what the circumstances.

Hope or despair: it's our choice. A good place to begin is to follow the exhortation in Philippians 4:8— think on good things. "Whatever is true, whatever is noble, whatever is right, whatever is pure, whatever is lovely, whatever is admirable—if anything is excellent or praiseworthy, think about such things." Focusing on anything negative will tear us down, not build us up. Again, what we think *is* crucial.

Faces

Faces . . .
    haunting
      hopeless
        helpless
Reaching out
Yet backing away.

Faces . . .
    wearing smiles,
    but beneath lie
      uncertainty
        loneliness
          alienation
            apathy.

Faces . . .
In a crowd;
Mistaking noise for laughter,
And elbows for hands,
And shoves for a pat on the back.

Father, help us see the heart,
And meet a need,
Fill a void,
Be a friend.
Don't let us drown in complacency
    indifference
        selfish preoccupation,
Snug in our circle,
Secure in our niche,
While those around us
Hear our words about
    love
        and
            compassion
Bounce off empty walls,
Without any more meaning
Than the headline on a movie magazine.

Amen.

For Further Meditation

> Be strong and take heart, all you who hope in the LORD (Ps. 31:24).

> But now, LORD, what do I look for? My hope is in you (Ps. 39:7).

> Why are you downcast, O my soul? Why so disturbed within me? Put your hope in God, for I will yet praise him, my Savior and my God (Ps. 42:5).

> But as for me, I will always have hope; I will praise you more and more (Ps. 71:14).

> You were wearied by all your ways, but you would not say, "It is hopeless." You found renewal of your strength, and so you did not faint (Isa. 57:10).

> Let us hold unswervingly to the hope we profess, for he who promised is faithful (Heb. 10:23).

Almost certainly the greatest problems plaguing mankind are guilt and shame. Their influence is widespread and the effects on all our lives is staggering.

— Dwight Carlson, M.D.

Guilt is like a dandelion: indiscriminate in its choice of soil, deep-rooted, and tenacious once sprouted.

— Mary Vaughn Armstrong

18

Guilt and Shame: Double Trouble

It doesn't take long for the chronically or frequently ill Christian to become devoured by guilt and shame. Consider the issues we're hit with: anger, grief, rejection, loneliness, depression, and faded hopes and dreams. No, we need not and should not be consumed with these characteristics and fears, but then that "body buffer zone" of the world of the well has been compromised for those who are afflicted.

Sadly, guilt and shame can be reinforced by the so-called "prosperity movement." The proponents of this movement teach that physical health is tied in to spiritual health. They remind us that we lack the faith to be healed or cured. It is a tragedy that those teaching this message, in their earnest eagerness to proclaim the fact that everyone can be well, are prolonging and/or worsening the afflictions of many due to guilt and shame. What are we doing wrong?

Scripture clearly stresses the fact that Christians will have trials and testings. We will be tried by fire—and most Christians are running around with a lot of smoke pouring out of them.

Yes, we are limited, different, and deficient in our capacity to perform. It seems shameful that often our first thought in the morning is, "How soon can I take a nap?" We watch our friends plan to storm like a whirlwind through their day!

Guilt and shame enter when we recognize our limitations—particularly if we once specialized in something we can no longer do. We feel we are outside the normal boundaries of society. We use a lot of energy to prove that we are just like everyone else. But we are not.

More guilt and shame appear when we think how we may be draining family finances, altering the schedules of some, and perhaps disrupting the lives of our friends.

We're to just "turn it over to God"; those fears anyway. It's another formula that can be frustrating. There is so much to turn over to him! In our affliction it is possible to turn the dilemmas over to God but then take them back. Everything is dear to us!

Sometimes the afflicted, barely coping with pain, exhaustion, depression, and frustration, can't turn things over to God as easily as if we were flipping hamburgers. More shame and guilt.

Shame and guilt will cause our physical and emotional symptoms to worsen. We will become bitter, not better. For every step forward, shame and guilt will set us two steps backward.

We must come to terms with the fact that *we* are *not* like everyone else. Our lives, either for a short or long period of time, are defined by our illness.

Truly it is life's biggest blow to embrace and claim Biblical admonitions, yet find ourselves still sick. Or claiming the promises, but then taking a turn for the worse. Praying knees become calloused. Hopes soar and fade.

Jesus never shamed those he healed. The Bible portrays him as a gentle-spirited man who truly grieved over people's affliction. He did honor the faith of many, such as the woman who had been hemorrhaging for twelve years. He took time. He had pity. But we don't see him laying guilt on those he touched. Jesus probably even healed some who were his enemies.

We are clearly living in a generation in which our lifestyles *promote* affliction. Stress, poor eating habits, smoking, drinking, drug use, and sexually transmitted diseases are rampant. For the latter, the Christian can feel not just guilt and shame, but demoralized, and defeated, and caught in a web of despair. After all, God destroyed whole cities for sexual sins.

The beauty of the cross is that Jesus' shed blood cleanses *all* of these sins if we but ask. Jesus hung there in agony so that *all* could find freedom from sin and guilt and shame.

Slow Down, World

Slow down, world!
Halt your maddening pace to and fro,
Going nowhere,
On the move, yet directionless.
Running frantic,
Pursuing elusive goals,
And leaving in the dust
A needy soul
Who wanted just ten minutes of your time
To listen.

Can't you hear the deafening roar of humanity
In need of just one person
Who will forsake the pursuit
Of fun and games for a day
And say, by listening,
"I love you."

Lord, in this generation
Which is in a time capsule
Set at fast forward,
Thanks for never moving,
For being consistent,
Reliable
And never-changing.

Amen.

For Further Meditation

> Submit to God and be at peace with him; in this
> way prosperity will come to you. Accept instruc-
> tion from his mouth and lay up his words in
> your heart. If you return to the Almighty, you
> will be restored (Job 22:21–23a).

> But he knows the way that I take; when he has
> tested me, I will come forth as gold. My feet have
> closely followed his steps; I have kept to his way
> without turning aside. I have not departed from
> the commands of his lips; I have treasured the
> words of his mouth more than my daily bread
> (Job 23:10–12).

> In my distress I called to the LORD; I cried to my
> God for help. From his temple he heard my
> voice; my cry came before him, into his ears (Ps.
> 18:6).

A "thorn in the flesh," "partaking in the suf-
ferings of Jesus," "joining all creation that
groans and travails," a "result of the Fall"—
the results are the same: a disrupted life.

—author unknown

There are so many "invisible diseases." Out-
wardly one looks well, but inwardly they are
devastated, frightened, confused, frustrated,
lonely and sick.

—author unknown

19

Twentieth-Century
Job's Comforters

One of our greatest losses is the loss of our friends. Sickness emphasizes flaws in our relationships, and we often struggle with conflicting feelings toward loved ones. It is not unusual for the most tenderhearted friends to have times when our problems seem too much for them. Because of our pain and discomfort, our resistance is down; this leads to anxiety, anger, fear, and more. Thus we can even become hostile to those who love us the most.

However, the disappearance of friends doesn't mean they necessarily love us less. Some just don't know what to say any longer in cases of chronic illness. They don't like to watch our suffering. Their own lives are cluttered to the hilt. They will continue to pray daily for us, but their presence may be scarce.

Illness throws relationships off balance. One person becomes more needy than the other. The even flow of give-and-take may not be so even!

Are we now more undesirable company? Has our appearance or personality drastically changed? Generally, if *we* are handling our affliction well, so will others. However, if we're always panic-filled and expressing morose pessimism, then a growing list of lost friendships may result.

However, at the same time there is a mounting list of "Job's comforters" at our doorstep. It should be stated that every "Job's comforter" wants us well. However, often their advice and formulas for us to get well, if we don't respond, could jeopardize the friendship. Many of their pious platitudes become flimsy Band-Aids that we want to tear off so our wounds can heal naturally. But the well-meaning formulas haven't changed throughout the centuries. We may be "hindering our own healing" in some way. We're to "confess our healing daily" and it will happen. We're reminded that "God never gives us more than we can bear" in spite of suffering that may be unspeakable. We're told that "God will give you a much greater ministry because of all you have gone through." A perplexing platitude and a dangerous one for new Christians states, "God must love you so much, he is allowing you to go through this terrible experience." We're told, "We all have our 'thorn in the flesh'" (though ours may feel like a sword). We're to "stand upon the Word of God" even on days when our brain simply cannot process anything from the Bible, a book, or a tape. Then there is, "Have you searched your heart for some secret sin?"

Strange and sometimes questionable suggestions are made. Certain areas of holistic health are pushed at us with money back guarantees. Vitamin therapy is the big push and it is fairly safe. Other areas are Chinese herbs blessed by Buddhist priests, acupuncture, reflexology, kinesiology, and much more. While proper nutrition is vital, it often seems that the advice given in this area will allow us to eat only vegetables, brown rice, and rice cakes that taste like styrofoam cups.

We probably don't need another book, tape, seminar, or experimental method for getting well. What we do need is love, patience, and kindness (notice I did not say sympathy). Dear friends, please pray for us. For while we are praying and waiting for a miracle, the world of the well can storm the gates of heaven with greater strength and endurance! Lend us a hug and a listening ear. Or send us a card that says we are loved just the way we are.

It is difficult for many who have not known serious illness to understand that certain problems just don't go away; nor do they fit a pattern or follow an agenda.

Affliction need not destroy friendships. If dealt with properly, on both sides, it can knit people together. And we must reflect back to when we were well. We didn't understand a lot of things either. We may have failed many a sick friend, though our intentions were pure and our desire to see them well pulled at our heartstrings.

Crash Course

Lord, something tells me
 I could flunk this course You're offering.
You're asking me to
 give myself away
 think on the needs of others
 restore life to the hurting
 put bandages on the wounded and
 rebuild those society calls unfit.
At the same time, You want me to
 crucify selfishness and ego
 deny my whimsical needs
 squelch all elements of pride
 and to basically forget about myself . . .
  not just for a day
  but forever!

I guess I need assurance, Lord,
That only God-breathed words will
emanate from my mouth;
That Divine love will motivate my actions;
That nonsense and trivia will be driven from
my thoughts,
And be replaced by meaningful thought and dia-
logue.

Father, forgive my doubting spirit.
Forgive me for thinking You are too small to
tear down
remake
rebuild
and restore
in Your image!

Amen.

For Further Meditation

Sacrifice thank offerings to God, fulfill your vows to the Most High, and call upon me in the day of trouble; I will deliver you, and you will honor me (Ps. 50:14–15).

On my bed I remember you; I think of you through the watches of the night. Because you are my help, I sing in the shadow of your wings. I stay close to you; your right hand upholds me (Ps. 63:6–8).

But as for me, it is good to be near God. I have made the Sovereign LORD my refuge; I will tell of all your deeds (Ps. 73:28).

Lay hold of my words with all your heart; keep my commands and you will live (Prov. 4:4).

I want to know Christ and the power of his resurrection and the fellowship of sharing in his sufferings, becoming like him in his death (Phil. 3:10).

Faith makes all things possible; hope makes all things bright; love makes all things easy — gratitude makes all things doubly beneficial.

—author unknown

20

An Attitude of Gratitude

The subject of gratitude saturates the pages of the Bible. There are literally hundreds of references dealing with gratitude and praise. We are to praise and thank God for his manifold mercies. But must we thank him for pain and affliction? Yes! There are promises connected with praise to, and adoration of, God, for all he is and does.

We are to thank him even for the unwelcome: "give thanks in all circumstances" (1 Thess. 5:18). The Bible also speaks about the "sacrifice of thanksgiving" (Ps.

137

116:17 KJV). This sacrifice of thanksgiving is necessary for the unwelcome things that come into our lives— like affliction. For despite affliction, our blessings are as numerous as the stars of heaven. Though many of us are going through a "wilderness experience," we must thank God that this world with its troubles, aches, pains, diseases, disappointments, and more, is *not* our home. Eventually our bodies will be made perfect. In eternity we'll need no prescriptions, exams, or surgeries. The hope of heaven is the *ultimate* hope for which we must be thankful. Sooner than we think, we are going to leave this world of sorrows.

Yes, we are to thank God even though our lives have been interrupted; even if the future on this earth seems bleak at times; even though our afflicted lives seem to have little purpose. Somehow God ordained that gratitude would produce contentment. It checks gloom, destroys envy, and returns with blessings on the head of the thankful one. We experience the sweetness of any divine mercy twice over when we are sincerely grateful for it.

As we pray, we must praise. Requesting further favors, we must remember past provision. Too often we approach God as beggars: "Give me, give me." We are so taken up with immediate cares, needs, and problems that we do nothing but request. We *take* all we can, but fail to satisfy God's bountiful heart as it yearns for the gratitude of those he blesses.

Perhaps there is no darker sin than that of ingratitude.

Small Miracles

Lord, how many miracles have I overlooked
  today?
Some of the greatest are the smallest . . .
  A snowflake
  A butterfly
  A colored leaf
  The fragrance of a flower . . .
Or, a smile from a friend on a mundane
  Monday.
A card received for no occasion,
But to tell me I was loved.
A squeeze of the hand.
A wink.
An arm around my shoulder.
Simple things.
Help me to listen to the silence, Lord,
And bask in the joy of simple things . . .
and the small miracles of life.

Amen.

For Further Meditation

> Come and listen, all you who fear God; let me tell you what he has done for me (Ps. 66:16).

> I will praise God's name in song and glorify him with thanksgiving (Ps. 69:30).

> How can I repay the LORD for all his goodness to me? (Ps. 116:12).

> Always giving thanks to God the Father for everything, in the name of our Lord Jesus Christ (Eph. 5:20).

> Do not be anxious about anything, but in everything, by prayer and petition, with thanksgiving, present your requests to God (Phil. 4:6).

The word acceptance is used to denote an optimistic, hopeful attitude. And yet affliction is seldom acceptable.

—author unknown

Coming to terms with a debilitating or chronic illness is almost like having a conversion experience.

—author unknown

21

Acceptance Doesn't Mean Giving Up

There are certain tragedies that one is able to accept more than intense short term or chronic illness. The everyday pain, fatigue, and a myriad of other symptoms remind us of their presence 24 hours a day. Here's where a "sacrifice of praise" is needed—even if the praise sounds a bit hollow. God knows we are trying.

It's much too easy for us to become preoccupied with our total dilemma. Thoughts can become obsessive. Everything seems out of control. Our bodies are out of control and rule us like a cruel taskmaster. Our limits and our lifestyles are difficult to accept.

What if God were to say in a still, small voice, "These are my sufferings . . . I am trusting you to go through this experience, even if I never tell you why. Can you do this for me?"

Grace and trust. They need to make a grand entrance. For the afflicted, getting through a day is simply the result of God's grace. Grace comes by way of trust. Trusting God means believing his purpose is higher and more important than our comfort and convenience. The question remains: "Who will allow God the Father to work out his larger plan?"

We can look back longingly for the life we once had. For many, it will return; for others, life will never be the same. Can we make the best of a less than ideal situation for today? Can we pray that serenity prayer: "God, grant me the serenity to accept the things I cannot change; the courage to change the things I can; and the wisdom to know the difference"?

Otherwise, thoughts of *what might have been* will torment us and increase our dilemma. We must grieve, let go, trust, and go on with our life. Or we can get stuck in the quicksand of self-pity, worry, envy, anger, frustration, and unanswered questions to the point where our symptoms only worsen.

Accepting our current situation doesn't mean giving up! It actually provides a base from which we can grow.

Often, at a point of acceptance, God's healing hand moves. But not always. Yes, our dreams were filled with grand expectations and what might have been. We wanted to make an impact on this world (and many of us have). Unless God allows us to be cured or healed, we must accept that not all our plans will come without a miracle. Thus to better reflect our present dreams and ideals, we set new goals. Scaled down goals. Goals once thought too low to be acceptable, for we were out to save the world. To make an impact. To really count. To be extraordinary.

Yes, it is possible to construct a life in the spaces between moments of dysfunction. But learning how to keep discomfort and dysfunction at a minimum may require trial and error as our symptoms flare and subside.

Sick or well, we really do matter. We do have significance. Our lives are daily being used of God. We are loved no less than when we were well, although admittedly there are awkward points.

It may be a battle, but then God can't go to war with an army of tin soldiers.

Jesus encourages us to give a cup of cold water to the hurting (Matt. 10:42). Even more so if we have experienced their pain and thus know how they feel.

Never has there been a generation like ours, so filled with thirsty people.

Lord, Set Me Free

Lord, set me free!
No, the bars are not of steel,
But rather chains of
   indifference
   conformity
   complacency
   and taking You for granted.
But seeking Your will and purpose requires
   motivation
   action
   stepping out of the routine
   changing direction perhaps
   giving up old habits
   changing a life-style.
That's hard, Lord.
I like to do things the same way.
I rebel at having to start over.

I rebel even more at having to say,
  "I'm sorry. I'll try again."

I don't want to be in a spiritual rut, Lord,
A victim of my own pride and stubbornness . . .
Taking baby steps toward spiritual growth . . .
With one step forward and two back.

Set me loose from myself, Lord,
A slave only to You,
In whom I have such wonderful freedom.

                    Amen.

For Further Meditation

When anxiety was great within me, your consolation brought joy in my soul (Ps. 94:19).

I will sing to the LORD all my life; I will sing praise to my God as long as I live. May my meditation be pleasing to him, as I rejoice in the LORD (Ps. 104:33–34).

Look upon my suffering and deliver me, for I have not forgotten your law. Defend my cause and redeem me; renew my life according to your promise (Ps. 119:153–54).

Those who trust in the LORD are like Mount Zion, which cannot be shaken, but endures forever. As the mountains surround Jerusalem, so the LORD surrounds his people both now and forevermore (Ps. 125:1–2).

Those who sow in tears will reap with songs of joy. He who goes out weeping, carrying seed to sow, will return with songs of joy, carrying sheaves with him (Ps. 126:5–6).

How God rejoices over a soul, which, sur-
rounded on all sides by suffering, does that
upon earth which the angels do in heaven:
namely, loves and praises God.

—G. Tersteegen

Let the pain you are experiencing be to you as
an untapped reservoir, a well of strength. God's
method of imparting wisdom is unconven-
tional according to the world's standards.

—Rich Wilkerson

22

"Love Is a Verb": Parting Thoughts

All who love us want to restore us; particularly the undershepherd who is a
spouse, parent, or other family member. He or she is
appointed by God to attend to our daily needs. Some
live elsewhere, but daily check on our needs. We
afflicted know you are dealing with a multitude of
intense feelings, too: inadequacy, impatience, anger,
fear, grief, denial, loss of your personal life, guilt perhaps, and more.

If you are a full-time undershepherd, you have lost freedom from a productive life, too. Your personal schedules and routines are altered. Relaxation, travel, even brief getaways may be things of the past. Your life is on hold just as much as the one for whom you are caring. But whether you have chosen the role or not, in a sense a loved one's life may rest in your hands. And it may be a monumental burden.

But God has handpicked you. He seems to help you find the whole person in our aching body and uneven emotions. You are at our side—perhaps not as much as we would wish—but enough so that the time is sacrificial.

It's your "language of love" that lifts us up. Even small gestures. Perhaps time spent listening; a flower; a card; a lunch if we're able. What we don't need is an abstract analysis of our problem, trying to discern just where we went wrong.

But we long to hear instead, "I love you;" "I really care how you're doing today;" "I'm here if you need me." Or from one who has also suffered, an "I know how it feels" is appropriate. Scripture verses (familiar ones) can be helpful, but in our deepest affliction may not be absorbed into our minds. Hopefully they penetrate our spirit and our heart.

Love is a verb, for the language of love is needed in word *and* deed.

The language of love listens. Then listens some more. Though there may be no answers to our dilemma, we need someone in our ordeal to help us sort out our thoughts, hopes, fears, dreams, expectations and more. In the process, you seldom utter pious platitudes. Listening is a skill not everyone has!

People with handicaps do need people—in spite of "pop psychology" that warns against co-dependency. That word should be tossed out when it comes to the afflicted. If we're isolated too long, we lose all sense of "connectedness" which is so important in keeping our mental health. If we can't get out, we depend on the outside world to come in.

We sometimes forget that it is God's love that is prompting undershepherds and others who care to act. He knows when we need a touch from "God with skin on." He knows there are many days when we're only able to lay back and be ministered to.

Actually, we may not know such quality of character in another until we hit such a crisis. Those we think might rally and exhort us, often disappear. Thus some undershepherds come out quietly from behind the curtain of our life, onto center stage.

And in our weakness or discouragement, the afflicted want to give back to you who love us and care. It is in giving that we receive, and there is healing in giving. Whoever is reaching out to us also needs to receive the ministry of *our* love and encouragement. You *do* need a sense of appreciation, for your lives have been disrupted. Appreciation that in the course of a day or a week, you have put us high on your agenda, perhaps interrupting your career, ministry, or personal needs.

We desperately need those of you who care, for

much of the world is focused on corporate profits and selfish needs. We want to tell you that we cherish every moment of time that you give us. God has put you on special assignment and that is to help love us back to life. We need you to help us focus on the rose and not the thorn. To help us see the glass half full and not half empty. To remind us of our blessings rather than what seem to be our cursings. To keep our minds not on the high cost of living but on the high cost of Jesus' dying—"with his stripes we are healed" (Isa. 53:5 KJV).

We know there are no easy answers. The rain falls "on the just and on the unjust" (Matt. 5:45 KJV). Those of you who love us, please remind us that under the beating of that rain are springing up spiritual flowers of such fragrance and beauty as never before grew in the unchastened life of ours. We see the rain; help us smell the flowers.

Tiny Sparrow

You out there . . .
Feathers ruffled with the wind and snow;
Perched on a branch
Nearly bent in two,
Clutching to it, calmly,
Swaying, almost in time
To the beat of the winter wind.

Why do you,
A tiny sparrow,
Peer into my window
And almost into my mind and heart?
What is it you would say
Should we communicate?

And if I should make a warm nest for you,
Would you leave your perch
And give up the winter chill?
I think not.

Yet you are speaking to me
Through your tranquility
　　steadfastness
　　and courage.
The sun shines now to warm your icy wings.
The wind and snow have ceased their cruel sting.
You jubilantly echo a new song . . .
"This storm God has seen me through.
Would He do less through the storms of life
　　for you?"

P. S.

Call me before you visit, but don't be afraid to visit. My lifestyle is a lonely one. I need to know people care.

Allow me to talk about my ordeal, but not to dwell on it. You can just ask me, "Do you feel like talking?" On some days we might not talk a great deal. We can sit silently together and I will feel comforted.

Encourage me. Help me feel good about my appearance in spite of my circumstances.

Talk with me optimistically about the future. Don't let me dwell on the past, and don't let me get caught in the "if only" syndrome, which adds to regret and depression.

Never let me lose hope. I may throw it on your shoulders now and then, but see that I return to it.

Touch me—put your arm around my shoulder, squeeze my hand, or give me a hug. It reinforces the fact that you care.

Bring me a spirit of laughter! You may have to draw me out of my shell, but help me to laugh . . . even at myself.

Offer to take me out now and then, but be cautious of my limitations.

Help my family. They are suffering in other ways and I cannot always attend to their needs.

Help me get through holidays. It may seem to me that the whole world is having one big celebration on special days. I feel so left out because of my circumstances. Don't let me fall into the "black hole" of discouragement and even despair during these occasions.

Offer to do minor housework. When laundry and cleaning pile up, I sink both emotionally and physically.

Share important news with me, lest I feel that the world is passing me by.

If you see something that pertains to my ordeal, please share it with me! I want to be tuned in to see how others going through the same or similar experience are coping and overcoming.

Now and then bring me (and my family) a taste treat. Many days I simply cannot even provide meals for my family.

Call ahead and see if I may have an upcoming transportation need. That provision will greatly lighten my load.

Share *your* ordeals with me! It is good to know that I am not the only one with affliction, disappointment, and shattered dreams. But more importantly, tell me how you overcame your "trial by fire."

Please be patient while I'm "on hold." So many won't stick around when the road gets rough.

Keep others informed about my condition. One can never have too many pray-ers.

If appropriate, weep when I weep.

Just tell me you love me. I feel like a burden to many. I need reinforcement and encouragement. I need to know that I am loved.